I hope my words bring you comfort, and if not, I hope they guide you toward the path you seek.

I want to thank my friend Makayla Danielle Adair, for always being there for me. The one who has inspired and motivated me to write this book.

DISBELIEF

I stretch your name
And entrap it in my words
So you stay intertwined
Between my fingers

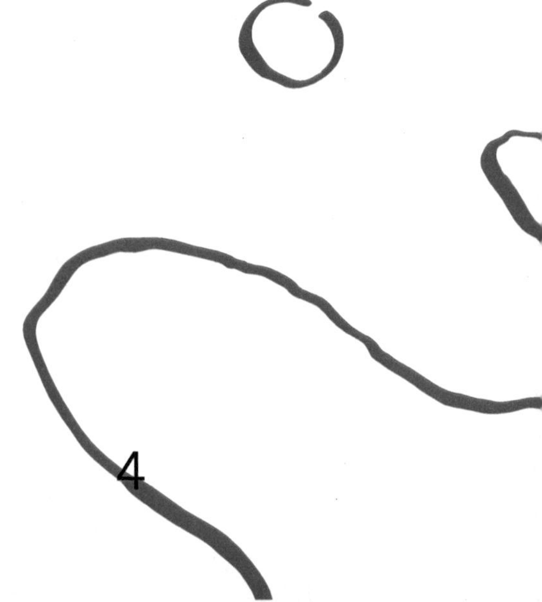

Dip my feet in your crimsons
My mind is violet for you
Drown me in your oranges
And lose yourself in my blues
Be my red
I'm your yellow
The first stab of love
Is sunset
A blaze of colours
To swim in
Paint me pink
And stroke me purple
Only in you
I see my shades
Only you can make me feel
White
Don't turn away from me
Be my mirror
I'm your light.

Every person you meet is a chapter. A universe that crosses path with yours. For a brief moment your fates entangle and then you let it go. People are experiences, each comes with their own color and paints your canvas. At the end of the book, you have a painting of your own.
Each person was a part of you all along, a mirror of a hidden part of you.

Forgive me then. I want to disrupt the book and end at your chapter. I don't want to turn the page, nor do I want any editions to it. Let me stay in your universe and let me entangle so deeply in you that the fate of a hundred people can't detangle ours. I want to melt in your color and paint the pages with the shade it forms. I want to only look into the mirror that reflects me you.
I want to be yours against all odds and warnings
I want to be with you despite it being the end of the world
I want to stop the time with you even if it means there's no future to see or past to reminisce. Do you want it too?

Piercing eyes
Your haunted gaze
Can tame the darkness of the underworld
And bring them down to their knees

Then how do you expect me to stay sane?
They make my tongue twist
And spirit loose
The yes sounds like a no
And the please spells exactly like a sorry
My head follows the movement of your order

You take my name
And my throat screams a no
But my voice whimpers a yes
Your eyes are hypnotizing
I can't help but
Surrender

Your gaze soft
And hold gentle
I wonder often
Do you fear breaking me
Out of love
Or a belief
That says I'm not yours to keep.
Hold me like
You've held me for lifetimes
Breathe your life into me
And let go.
I'll always have love for you
All my lifelong,
All yours too.

My fever dream,
My glimpse of paradise,
The love of my
Some previous lifetime
My fingers are shivering
To grip your silhouette
Trade my lifetime of joy
For some more minutes of this tenderness

Take my breath away
My back fragile, and soul weak
In front of your Venus smile
I won't be able to outlive your departure
I'm not ready to see you
Slipping away.

Love feels
Different to each part of you
The eyes taste
The color of roses
Your heart feels
The taste of sunflowers
Your soul loves the flavor of lilies
And your feet rest in jasmines

The melodies look different to each
But they all define it
As you.

Love sits in your chest, as if you've gulped an infinite of sunlight in a second. Your heart shines and throbs like a star birthing it's own universe. Your ribs weaken. Soul melts.

Love sits in your chest like you've finally drank a drop of the holy elixir. In that second you see, why the Demons and Gods fought with each other. Why the heavens and hell would collide against each other.

Love reminds you of your childhood. That one evening, you were just a child, enjoying a carefree life. A child running and playing. A child who just ran home and drank the first glass of water gasping. Your whole body filled with oxygen in a second.

What do you do then? When love turns poisonous. When love starts bleeding. When love starts to feel fatal. An elixir not to be consumed by you? How do you stop something that has already taken over you?

Paint me Red
And name me yours.
Cage my body
Then claim my soul

Peel open my skin
Layer by layer
And entangle your veins with mine
Announce the official
Declaration of your love

You're mine
And i'm yours
Scream at the heavens above
And drag me straight to hell

Infringe the laws of the lords
And possess my body with
Your blasphemous soul
Ravel your heart with mine
And sink into me

When there's us
There's no you
There's no me.

You are the glorious heir
Of the throne of hell
The ash of evil
Imbedded in your being
You sink in your sins
While i stink of your skin
I'm a sloth submerged in your energy
Chained to this maddening desire
I envy the free
While I drip in this indulgent greed
Such wrath I hold in my eyes for you
That it translates into pride
You've dragged me through this hellfire
My netherland named after you
I've surrendered my sanity
And sacrificed a life of virtue
Now drown my soul in your sins
And show me what true liberation is.

I'm not yours to keep
But hide me away
Let me live a little life
Love a little lie
Put me in a trance
My favourite daydream
Let me in thoughts at least
Weave us a perfect tale
Help me runaway with you
Help me take refuge in you
Will you fight fate
With your tooth and nail
To lose to destiny
Just for me?

The ache of almost
Is the womb I hide in
It's my mother's voice
That now puts me to sleep
The bonds of heart
Unthread in my hands
Tired of sewing them back
They only grow thinner
I weave a blanket of all that's lost
And sleep under it.

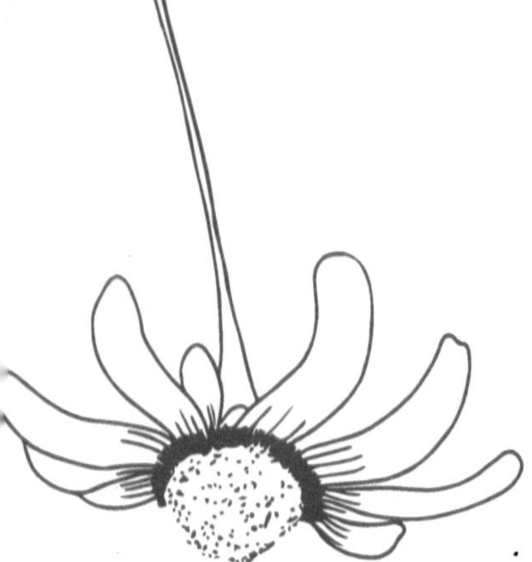

You love for a second
You remember it a lifetime

DENIAL

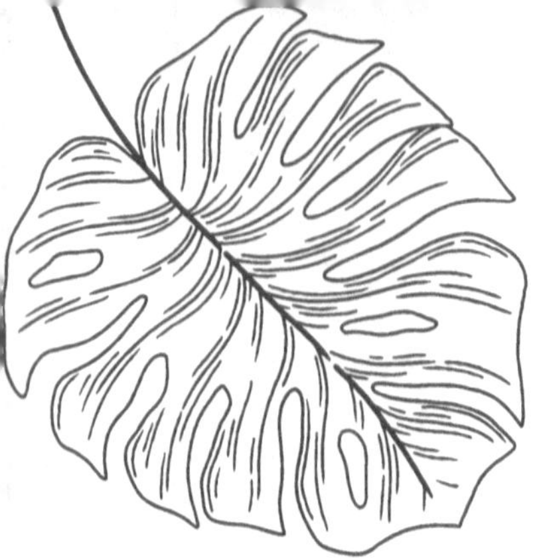

Unveil my every scar
And find your name inscribed there

You say
We are tied by the rope of fate
It's love
We can never let go of each other
The push and pull
Will remain
Even when the skin on our palms
Is worn out

I'm already exhausted
You see
At the end of the rope
I'm always giving
Giving
And giving
Till there's none left in me

You ask me
Why I look so pale
And have I not been eating lately?
Have I not been taking care of myself?
How could you be so blind
To the consequences of your own actions?

I tell you
That my limbs are tired
And my knees hold no strength
That I might want to let go
This string of fate
That maybe I dont believe in it
That I'm tired
That I want to save myself before it's too late

You chuckle
And show me your rigged palms
Regret instantly sews my throat
Then you push me on my back
And pull me back up
I hold myself still
To grasp some air
To breath
To stay

You tell me
That my back, my spine
Is still as strong
I show you my palms
The skin, the flesh is almost gone
You can see my bones
You can see how I'm trying

I'm trying
From my every root
To catch up with you
And hold this rope
You chuckle
Once again

And take the rope out of my hands
I'm free
I think
No!
Before I can even relax my fingers
You put the rope
Around my neck
It's a leash!
I say
No!
It's the rope of fate
You say
And drag me away
From sanity and myself
The truth is
You're dragging me
Over a sharp knife

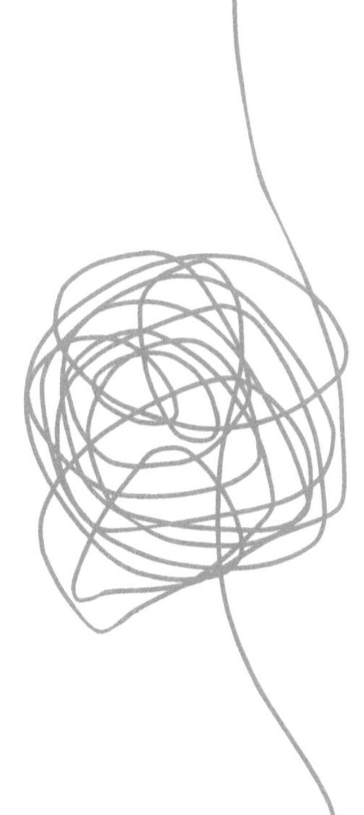

To a place unknown
Slitting my every part
It satisfies you
To see me in pain
And call it fate
But this is love
And love
Is the most violent act in the world
So even when blood is dripping down
My entire body

I see your face
And its contentment
And I shut my cries
And smile
Upon this walk
Upon this drag
To death
It's too late to save myself anyway
So I see
How much more flesh to destroy?
How much blood to drain?
I smile
I look at you
And call this
My fate
You.

Longing is a poison; it is meant to destroy you slowly and painfully. Longing tortures you with occasional hope, and frequent dreams.

Longing has a sharp sting. It carries a weak blade that keeps striking you at every breath. You keep bleeding drop by drop, neither do you live, nor die.

Longing smiles at your suffering and promises you unreal futures. You lose yourself every second you spend with it. It takes over you, one day at a time.

Longing bites your heart and poisons it. Longing wants to isolate you from your own life and build a room for just you two.

Longing will kill you; it will comfort you while it poisons you to death. Run before it engulfs you. But will you able to?

Teach me
How to be a stranger again
My hopes and dreams have left me
To build a home in ocean eyes
The bricks are made from
Bittersweet memories
And walls stand on
Wishes together
The roof is white
And windows huge
My soul stands at its door
And loses itself in its beauty
But I fear it wont
Withstand your sea storms
Or wicked dreams.

Red takes over my vision
It is all I can see
The red string of fate
Binds me to you
The faith
Stitching your soul with mine
From several lives
Since the beginning of time

An eyeball to an eyeball
A finger to a finger
It goes around my neck, wrapping your throat
My navel roped to yours
My heart strapped across yours
Each strand of hair in a braid with yours
My soul fusing with yours

The ruling of the divine
Cannot be denied
I've accepted this fate
But why do you turn pale
Holding scissors in your hand?

All the things
That keep me humane
Are inhumane.
My ache for suffering
My taste for pain
My desire for agony
Comfort in the discomfort
And choice of torment
All the things
That keep me humane
Are you humane.
You

Your love stands with mine
In the middle of an infinite ocean

Mine is a child
With an untainted heart
And open palms
Oozing life
Ready to pour unconditionally
Ready to give undoubtedly
Ready to love

Yours is a weary grave keeper
A grim reaper that denies death
With a worn out heart
And rotten fingers
Shoulders carrying heavy caskets
And hands holding various shades of grief

You and I
Stand in the middle of the eternal sea
Hands in hands
Fingers interlocked
But the weight of your love
Is heavier than my faith
It's taste
Sweeter than my life
So I strap my feet together
And fall on my knees
My head underwater
Readily receiving
Death by devotion.

This battle with fate
Wrapped in desperation
I'm in a tug of war with god
I've to keep you as mine
Ive to keep you besides
I've to tie a knot in time
You and me
Stuck in on one side
I scream and shout
Lose my hands and lose my mind
How do we still end up on either sides?

I'm a soldier
At war with God.
My fingers clawing
In his back
Fists ripping off
His Angel wings
His skin shredded
Blood resting underneath my rusted nails
I've picked out my each tooth
To fight for you
My eyes tired
My face with blemishes
And throat with scars
My skin has been burnt
And stripped away
Bones visible and decayed
Why can I not see
We are not on the same side
It's not God, my enemy
It is you.

There's a melody that haunts me
A distant calling
A broken tune
And it sings
"Empty people cannot love"
So I pour and pour and pour
I'm not ready to see the empty in you.

GUILT

I'm clinging onto your silhouette
It's slipping off of me
Blaming you of haunting me
While all I want
Is to be haunted by you

Devotee of misery
I lie when I say
I believe in God.
There's no Lord I trust
Only bliss in suffering
It's an endless cycle
One that begins with me
And ends at the
Foot of torment
You'd want to save me
But be no fool
I come here willingly
There's no salvation
Like the one hidden in
Melancholy.

Loving you,
Is an offence against God.
It awakens the sinner inside me,
When our fingertips touch.
I can see the pits of hell,
In your almond eyes,
The fire of hell,
Carving a home inside my ribs.
Its every demon
Screaming inside my throat
And the Devil's smile
Residing in yours

Loving you
Is going to be the end of me
Stuck in the trenches of hell for an eternity
But how can I call it hell?
If it's with you
I call it home.

You settled so deep,
Into me,
I had to drag you out.
From the pit of my stomach
But my heart
Just won't let go.

So I bruised my lungs,
And broke my ribs,
To get rid of you

But you only dissolved.
More into my blood
Took over my skin
Now
I cannot even breathe
Without being H A U N T E D
By you.

I trim and tame my roots.
I want to run away farther,
Settle into the abyss,
Somewhere you have never heard of.

I want to establish myself,
So far from you.
No wind that ever caressed your skin,
Could come greet me,
But every time they grow

They head towards you.

It's demonic,
The grip you have,
Over my heart.

One too massive,
To rest in your palms.
It's dehumanising
The hunger I yet
Have for you.

The craving to be held
In your wire fences,
With electric shocks,
It's disgusting,
To see my heart,
Squirm and Squint.
Desperately,
Trying to fit into your hands.

Willingly,
Lovingly,
Cutting off parts of itself,
To mould into the shape of your fists.
Shamelessly,
I've turned into a madman.
Draining my blood myself,
To not weigh down your arms.

You toss me out,
And I crawl back to you.

You've shackled my feet
To the rocks and crusts
In the ends the ocean
Some mistakes can never be undone
And some ties can never be cut
Your name is a leash I cannot seem to remove
One the world cannot see
One that I help to hide
No matter how far across I've swam
How fast I've ran
How many ships I've crossed
And how many seas I've met
Your name spelled
Even once
Drags me down
And thumps me to the bottom of the world
Thumps me to the ground at your feet

The curse of Medusa
Has been confined
In your eyes
A thousand hungry snakes
Venomous tongues
And wicked resolutions
Starving for my lovesick heart

I'm no Persues
And you're not meek
Your eyes have engulfed my vision
And your venom is running in my blood
My feet can't turn away
My soul has already sank into the soil
You've turned me into a stone

Destruct me down to nothingness
And walk out of the crime scene
How can you not?
Afterall only I know
You're no victim of the sea
But Poseidon himself.

Brush and bath
A corpse
Beg the heavens
To bring it to life.
I've brushed the walls
With vinegar and blood
And whispered to Gods
I don't believe in.
Desperate for your
Return.
Retrospecting the
Repair this rebound
Will require.
I would rather
Sacrifice my soul
Than to lose
You.

Womanhood is a grief.
You mother the
Ancestral agony
Of every woman
Before you
Feed it beliefs
Meant to chain you
And tie it to the
Roof of your being.
You carry the guilt
And raise the ordeals.
The world stands by
To see your valour
And appreciates
Your submission
Dare not deviate
Only demons do.
I carry this weight
And do not wish to be
The ideal woman
Where do I abandon this child?
One this world leashed me to.

A list of all the things you should know if you ever fall in love with me

1. I've never known to trust, to rest. I've always had my one foot out of everything.
2. There are days when I can't even sit with my own self let alone anybody else.
3. I run away at the first sight of desertion. I run and isolate, and that's how I've kept myself safe.
4. I love to love people. I pour till it disgusts them.
5. I've never known what it means to detach and likely never will.
6. I sink into my feelings quick and refuse to let go.
7. I say I love love, but I'm still a stranger to it.

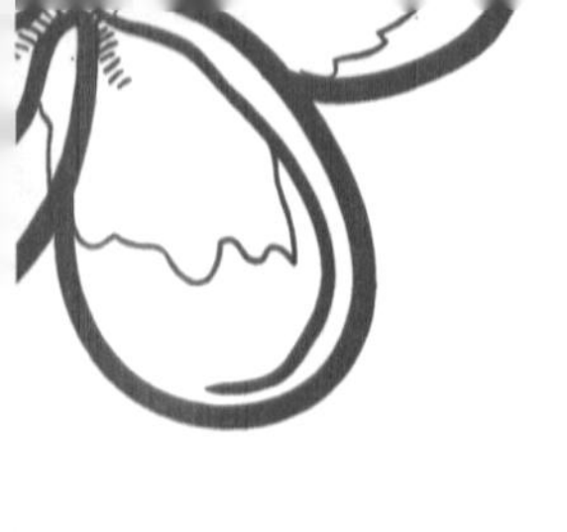

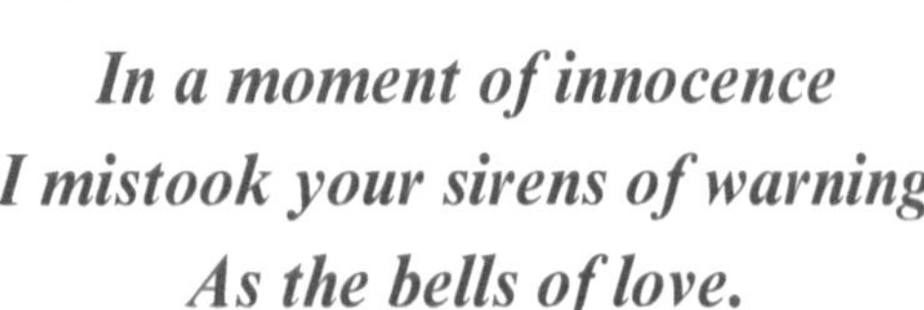

In a moment of innocence
I mistook your sirens of warning
As the bells of love.

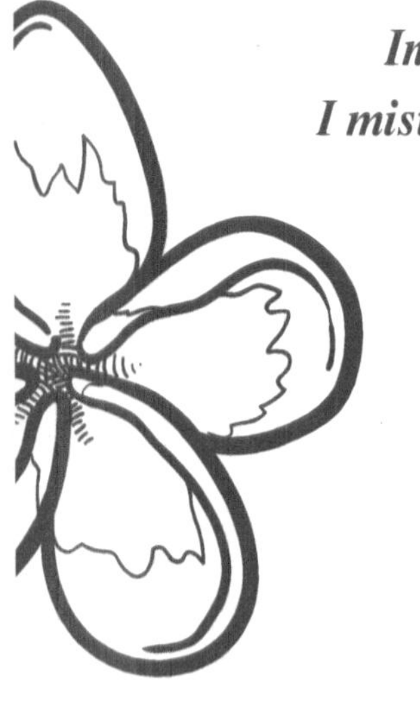

BARGAINING

There lies a void in my chest
Where once I sat with love
Mornings and evenings
I spend mending it
But no thread fits

There's a graveyard
Of dreams I visit everyday
where I've buried
The mirages of us
And bid them
Farewell
But tonight
Let me resurrect them
Draw me your fantasies
And rewrite our story
There are no second chances in life
So let me dive in our delusions
In death.

Tie my hands down
And make me sit down at your alter
Tattoo your name
On my eyes
Scleras chanting your name
Irises imitating the routes of your veins
Pupils morphing to look exactly likes yours

Paint your picture
Beneath my eyelids
Let my life be taken over
It's in vain
If it's not frantically devoted
To you

I’ll skin myself alive
To lay down a floor for you
Break my arms and legs
To build a staircase for you
Stretch out my veins
To decorate this house for you
My palms on the ground
To be your doormat
Ready to welcome you
My blood as paints on the wall
My bones on fire to keep you warm

I’ll sacrifice the whole of me
If it means
You'll build a home in me.

I’m begging you

Why don't you meet me?
When I've lost my senses
Of Right and Wrong.
Want and Need,
Desire and Detest.
When I can't runaway,
Or try to tie you down to me

Why don't you meet me
When I don't hate myself
To want you
So bad
When will that be?

My ears fall deaf
To sour words
Meant for you

If it's not your voice,
They shut down

My skin turns pale
And my eyes lower their gaze
I cant speak
If it's not about you

But you're not here
You never are

How much longer
Does this wait last?

I'm exhausted
Always being submerged in suffering

Time apart from you
Feels like poison being shoved down
My throat

And this ceaseless distance
Spoon feeding me agony

Run and return
Rescue me.

In my dreams
You stand in front of me
With your arms wide open
And hands of a sculptor

In my dreams,
You sit in front of me
With your eyes full of love
And fingers coated with tender touch

In my dreams
You're carving a woman
Out of me
One that is made
In your dreams.

One that makes you stay.

There's no cure in your comfort
Only relief in madness
Don't preach me peace
Be my muse, my symphony
Awaken me
Unleash me
Touch me
And show me my true self
A lunatic
Show me the mirror
You're me and I'm you
Touch me
Like I've never lived a life here
Unknown to this gaia
One look
And align my soul
Life, all lived and ever will live
Shatter this illusion
And liberate my soul
Show me
The truth
The religion
The God
You.

The mortal world
Accepts one trail
While demonizing the other
The unknown and bent
The forbidden path
Of the sacred
You're my unlawful instinct
My intrinsic intuition
My kismet's calling
You're the lie
For whom I shut down
The truth
At the rights and wrongs of the world
You stand at the corrupt
And i run to wherever you are
The world's virtues never belonged to me
Only you did.

Growing up clairaudient, I could always hear bells ringing. Soft music in the back of my life, always guiding me through life. As the old tales go, I thought these are my angels and guides connecting with me. But they never carried any words, only tunes of the divine. They ring and ring and ring and fade away. But when I saw you, and our eyes met. For the first time, I knew exactly what they meant. Perfectly aware of the meaning they carry.

But I was wrong all along and so were the tales. No angels exist, only demons with their warning signs.

My heart
Aches
for the day
When our eyes meet but slip off
As pure
strangers.
We don't
Look at each other
With heartbreak
Anymore,
Wondering If that's the
Person we
Loved or left?

I hope I never see your face again
While you're haunted by mine.
May time erase your name
While mine is forever inscribed in your mind.

REFLECTION

Run away, run as fast as you can
But running from yourself is an endless cycle.
Run and Run and Run. Then stop, sit down, and ask yourself.
What are you really running from?

I've been a stranger to myself. Always busy being someone else, always trying to please someone else. I've never met myself, only seen me through various mirrors. I've met the perfect daughter, the one that does her best to please her parents. Yet, she occasionally fails. I've seen the friend. The one that runs to others rescue, while she drowns in the blues. I've met the lover, the one that gives till there's nothing to give and doesn't take an ounce back.

I've met all these girls and know nobody. I've seen all these girls and like none. Who am I beyond the roles of the world. Who am I when I'm not filling the shoes of these characters? If my true self stood in front of me, would I recognize her?

I'm sick of always,
Laying at the foot of your temple
While you rest in your barren glory
Forehead touching the stairs
Of your false being.
Eyes wearied of yearning
Chest aching of despair
You've turned me into
A troubled devotee of
The dust
A vagabond,
Begging for your grant.
You're a nobody,
But you've stripped me of
My dignity.
Why do you stand so high?
And only reach down
To trample over me?

Love rests on my neck,
Adorned with a cursed chain.
Jeweled with,
Three ill-fated stones:
Passion, Devotion, and Obsession.

Passion binds me to hell
Only to pierce my eyes
And blind me out.

Devotion brings me down to my knees
Shackles my spirit,
And slow poisons me
While I lose my head
And blur my senses.

Obsession watches in awe.
Its hunger grows,
It lives,
To see
The morbid death
Of my soul.
Only to scream more

Why do I love,
The love
That hates me?
Love that loves:
Torture.
Love that spells out:
Pain.
Love that,
Loves that,
It's not written in my palms.
Yet, I irrevocably,
Love it.

An enemy
At the door of my chest
Guarded by my ribs
And concealed by the skin
This heart
Produces its own poison
One drop at a time
To spell your name
Which alchemist dares to see?
And which God great enough
To save the one
With a self written fatal fate?
No relief can occur
And no antidote can arrive
These hands have holes
And your love only slips away.

The faith of the Lunatic
Is love
A beloved menace
A cult for the masochists
A refuge for the tortured
The fate of the Lunatic
Is love
Hands holding the weight of wait
Eyes only familiar with longing
And head under the sea of misery
Breathless for the Liberation of soul
While being chained to the ground

The fallen are the lost cause
Love is not the religion of God
Striving for peace
It's a lie
Love is the dust devil
Worshipping death.

I built cathedrals for your love
Only for you to call it unholy
Ungodly. Irreligious. Irrelevant.

What a fool I must be
To offer redemption
To your blasphemous soul
You've mastered
The corrupt
And live as
The skilled trickster
But the tide changes,
No more will I
Abandon myself for you.
And no more will I
Leave out
My orphaned petals
In the pond.

I cannot turn away
From the sounds
Of my heart anymore
Collecting all my pieces
I'll lay out
An imperfect medley
Perfectly made for
Me.

How does one love themself? Where does it all begin? To love yourself, it must not mean to look the most beautiful. To spend tons on your make up, your clothes, your body and your beauty.

Where does it begin? Does it mean to be the smartest in the room? The silliest? The proudest? Or the bravest?

How do you love yourself?

Well, the first step is to accept yourself. As you are. With your flaws and blemishes. With what you consider your best and worst.

1.Stand in front of the mirror and point out every feature you don't like. Memorize that part of yourself. Now revisit it every day in front of the mirror. Look at it every day. Let yourself be uncomfortable to the point of comfort.

2. List out all your failures and celebrate them. Write an apology letter to your past self for not being there for yourself. Write a letter to every version of yourself that is crying itself to sleep over something that will not matter in future.

3. Do something without trying to improve. Why do you always want to be perfect? Do something for your heart, for your peace. Do it because you enjoy it, not because you want to perfect it. Everything in life is not a conquest to be won. A proof of your worth. Don't be desperate to master life, take a break and live it.

4. Give your inner critic a name and fight for yourself. That little voice in your head that loves to hurt you? Give it a name and talk back! Fight with it every time it wants to hurt you. Stand up for yourself, first to your own self.

4. Don't fear failing and don't fear embarrassing yourself. You do not remember the failures of others, and neither will they remember yours. Don't rob yourself a future of happiness because scared to be seen.

5. Spend time with yourself. Make a "Dear Me" scrap book, make a playlist, ask yourself the silliest questions, maintain a journal. Spend time with yourself. Love begins with true recognition.

6. Hug your inner child. Go back in time and remember every time you were crying as a child. All the harsh things that were said to you and go back in time. Hug your childhood self and comfort it like you needed it. Cry it out and love yourself regardless.

All my devotion turns violent
My love stinks and desire obsesses
I soak my feet in delusions
And lose my head to limerence
All my devotion turns vicious
I've never known people
And never seen any faces
I only paint
I sketch pictures for the neverland
And lose myself in it.
All my devotion turns poisonous
My madness is carefully
Chained to my existence
My loyalty to it is my prison
All my devotion rots
It sickens me
But I can't see it
It consumes my sanity
But it's my haven
Are you venomous?
And do you hate me like I hate myself?
Let me paint us a picture then
Let me be devoted to you.

It's a fabrication
I cannot accept yet escape
I run in circles
Nearing the end of this mirage
Crying and begging
To be freed from this looming entity

I'm being haunted by your ghost
Bedevilled by your spirit
Prayers are futile
And wishes are delusions

Summon the heavens
And call upon the Gods of the Universe
Which exorcism do I need
Which priest is the most capable
To get rid of such a demon
Even the devil is in awe of.

Anger on you
Is like a mother enraged.
A burst of emotions out of frustration.
A plea for mercy.
A cry that relieves.
How it comes from the pit of her stomach,
But doesnt last long,
It is her truth.
But not truer than her warmth
Weary screams while eating lunch,
But then her arms open
With unconditional love
Sitting by the dinner table.

Grief is the child of lost time and regret, it masks itself as anger. It stings and stitches your throat, but grief is still a child. Love it out of its anger and pain. Love it and see it bloom into content.

RECONSTRUCTION

The sky seems to be on fire
When your eyes are burning
Your hands ask for support
Destruction answers.

Love, why don't you be my love and not my teacher. I'm tired of sitting across this shabby dinner table, repeating the same lessons. Learning and unlearning the same scriptures. You're teaching me words I don't understand in a language that now seems foreign to me.

You've smacked my hands red and killed my appetite. There's only so much I can do. You leave every morning only to return at noon. You want to name me learnt but I'm only diligent. I diligently sit and write your name, everyday again and again yet always wrong. There's only so much you can do.

Love, when will you be my love and not my teacher? The plates have piled up, and my tears have too. Are we waiting to see who gets up first? A lifetime might not be enough for your enormous lessons, can we continue in the next? I need some peace. Love, let me rest.

The wind has passed
The message of your arrival
The autumn leaves
Have turned red and grey
Have withered and scattered
In the morning itself
Waiting for you to come

The clouds have cleared
And have asked the rain
To come some other day
For today, they want to admire you
The birds have been singing
Ever after they heard your news
And the sky is painted
In your colors and shades

Today the Sun hasn't left
For it has heard wonders about your face
And the moon has come early
For it has heard stories of your grace
They are all waiting
Only for you

Hiraeth

It's been so long
The trees have now stopped
Whispering your name
And the squirrels are now tired
Yet each one of them
Is pinching themselves to stay awake
To get a glace of you

Tell me
Just how am I supposed to
Tell them you're not coming
Not today
Tomorrow
Or ever?

You never even intended to.

I didn’t realize
When did I leave my grip on it
When did I exactly lose it?

Once I had love
Right in my hands
On the tip of my tongue

Now,
Love feels like a
Foreign word
A distant dream
That I once saw
Maybe, in a previous
Lifetime.

You say,
Ever after I left you,
The shores remind you of me,
The waves,
Calmly touching your feet,
And waving back.
Your heart,
Eases by its touch.
You say,
I remind you of ocean waves,
Always making you long for more,
Always making you want it to reach further,
Further than your feet.
Further than just skin.
I wonder,
How could I have done that?
When there's where you always placed me?
When there's where I always placed myself?

I fear
My life will always
Feel like this
A revolving door
With no break for pauses
Running in endless circles
Breathless

And between these
Delayed halts
My tired eyes
Rush and yearn
For your glimpses.

But I'll let the doubts be
And face my fears
I've fought harder battles
And dealt with deeper wounds
And if I get scared
I can run back home
And this time,
Run back to myself.

I sit at the shore of the sea and weep. The waves run to me with love in their arms and I hide myself in the castle of sand. Why do I do that? I stand at the shore of the sea and see the rays of the sunshine. I know one step ahead will bless me with the warmth of the Sun, but I run and run and take refuge in the shadows of the trees. Why do I hate myself? Who taught me that I can't have it all?

I want to soak my feet in water, but the sea salt burns my skin. I sit at the shore of the sea and weep. There's this boundary I cannot cross. But why?
I stand at the doorstep of love but can't climb the stairs of trust. The knob of my heart is rusted but the room inside still awaits. I stand at the shore of the sea and ask myself. How do I step into the light?

A wish
Is a glimpse into the future
Wishful hearts
The universe befriends you

ACCEPTANCE

But love comes in a million forms and shapes. Don't you be the fool that recognizes only one. Look around and lose yourself in every form it embraces you.

Where did you pick up this idea from? That you're whole only when you have a romance to be envious of? That you're lonely till you don't have someone's arms to fall into?
Why is love only glorious when it's romantic? Why do we think that all fairytales end with eternal love?

Snow white didn't meet love when the prince kissed her awake, rather when the dwarfs took care of her unconditionally. It was love when the birds sang to her daily and it was love when the animals wanted to caress her lovingly. Had she not met the prince, would you say she never knew what love?

And why do we think that the beast showed belle what love is? Belle knew love from the second she was born. Love was in the form of books she cherished, and the knowledge she earned. She knew love when her father risked his life to get a rose for her, when the teacups and cupboards loved to laugh with her.

Love is the most purposeful act of a human life. What we live for and will willingly die for. Then why do we cage it to only one form?

Don't you see? You were never alone. Never not loved. You too, were always surrounded by love.
That friend who loves drinking coffee with you? Loves you.
That cousin who laughs with you? Loves you.
Your mother who makes your favorite dessert every birthday? Loves you.
Your father who always ensures you have everything you need? Loves you.
Your sibling who pretends to be annoyed by you? Loves you.

Could you ever again say? That you're not loved?
People come and go, but love remains. Love you received and love you gave away.

You've always known love my dear, you're love.

My dear dear girl, don't you want to coat the whole world with love?
Your heart is full of colors, a melody of paints. It’s flowing out of your heart, and you want to hand it to every hand that touches you. But aren’t you so tired?

You keep painting the world yellow while it drowns you in blue. How did it feel when you first felt the thorns of blue? Fell into the depth of gray and the teeth of Maroon? My dear dear girl, with her hands full of love; don’t let the shadow of grief take over you. Don’t hide your light or drain your darling dyes.
Wear your scarlet heart on your sleeves, adorn it with jewels you keep giving away.

Enamel your palms with golden and pearl and apply it all over yourself. Give it to yourself, what you keep handing over to others. Give it to yourself, what you so dearly want somebody to give you. Don’t you see? You already have it all. The salmon, the rose; the apricot, the gold. Show me how you make your plum and where do you store your jade.

Sink into your own heart and walk out into the world. Paint the world as you please, let it see your every shade and let it shy away, but don't you walk away. Brush the whole world because you are abundant and not because you want somebody to see your palette. My dear dear girl, with hands full of love, why don't you give it to yourself first?

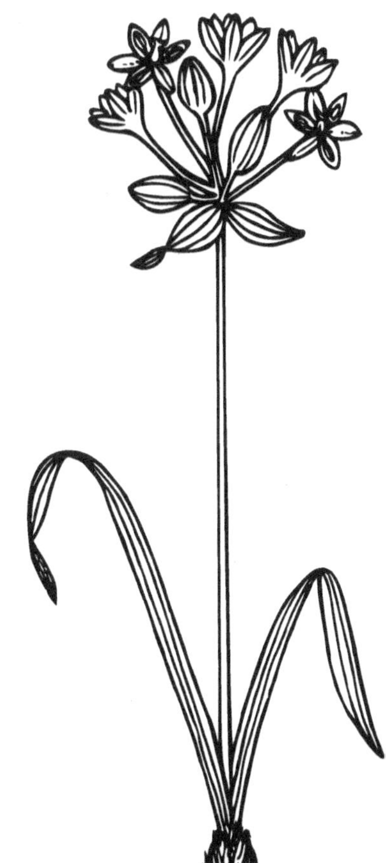

You left your pieces in me
I thought with time
They would disintegrate
And leave
But no!
They grew
Your every part grew into a whole you
And now you're caged in my heart
Every time your name falls off my tongue
Your pieces come alive
And long to go home
I understand
They weep and weep and weep and weep
And bang the walls of the prison they know
But I didnt intend to trap them in
And when they are tired banging
Hungry and crazy
They feed on my heart
I feel less alive
Every time I take your name
It's okay
The parts of you
The heart of you
I own, I say

And let you feed on me
Till it hurts me
And I'm gasping for air
It's okay
I'm sure
You're missing the parts of you too
You wish they would come back to you
And I want you to feel alive again too
Deep down,
I want to follow them
To home,
Theirs and mine.
Where love lives and home resides
But it took me more than hurt and pain
More than just wounds and breaks
To learn that
This body I'm born with
Is the only home I'll ever truly have
So next time
When my heart hurts
And I know you're calling for the parts of you
Caged right in here
I won't call it love and embrace the pain
I'll dive deep in me
And find the key, for the both of us.

The cost of becoming
Is often the life known
Alchemy befriends you
With a price to pay
Are you ready to lose?

Change is not your loving mother
It is the patriarch
That will strip you away
Of all you've ever known
A skin will be shed
And lessons will be learned
Every card is turned
And resistance becomes a paralyzed power

Piece by piece you evolve
Time will be the proof
Of your new
Inevitable mosaic.

And what if I tell you that you were correct all along. The person whose eyes pierced your heart, and glance hypnotized your soul was your soulmate. The person that flew you to the moon and pushed you down, indeed loved you in the soul. When you broke your limbs in hell and cried yourself to sleep in its fire. When you could see your nightmares in every mirror and dreams crushed under your own feet. When you forgot your own self and had to build a person from the scratch. It was all love, all along.

What is a soulmate if not someone who shows you the deepest trenches of your soul? Isn’t that what a soulmate does? Bring out the best in you by showing you the worst first? Would you have changed if they had stayed? Would you have ever recognized your own strength? Met your strongest self?

That was indeed your soulmate, the one who broke your heart. Whose name sounds like a knife right through your heart. God wouldn't choose a stranger for a lesson so important. For a turn so life changing. For a pain that will run so deep.

In another life, somewhere in another universe, you're laughing with them. Hand in hand, you're playing in a playground, plucking flowers in a garden, choosing a sweet name for each other, or wishing you could just steal another day with them.

In another life, maybe you're teaching them a harsh lesson. Showing them a life they don't even want to think of, holding their hand through the turmoil of life, or maybe being the reason for it.

But the person that broke your heart, whose thought feels like a bullet through your heart, is indeed your soulmate.

In the deepest corners of your souls, you trust them. You love them, and only they could teach you a lesson so deep.
So find it in you, to forgive them. Find it in you, to let it go. Forgive yourself and then forget them for this lifetime. Afterall, that is still a soulmate.

The dirty streams cleared,
And the rusted petals,
Withered and disappeared.
With the wind,
Leaving with the cold,
The light was not dead,
The soil still alive.

And just like that.
the new parts,
They bloomed,
With no blood,
Of the old.

I turned into a ghost and haunted you
Blew myself away,
Just to hover over you.

Your demons and mine
They come from the same depths of the underworld
Made of the same soil
Pieces of the same soul
It's not me
It's them.
That can't keep me away from you,
But I give that life away
And I surrender that part of me

The swords I've picked
To fight with fate
For you
I drop now
And set myself free.

I've found myself now.
Entangled in the metaphors of life,
Dare enslave my magic.
I’m the mystic,
From the dreamland.
I induce the trances,
That grasp your mind and blind your vision.
I'm the one for whom it rains,
And to whom the heavens bow.
Watch me as I unfold,
Watch me as I rise,
My page has been turned.
And the greatest poetry ever,
Has now been written.

Watch the roses bloom
Where even weeds fear to be.

Thank you for your valuable time.

Hiraeth is my debut book. A journey of self-belief and the courage to follow my heart's calling.

This book will always hold a special place in my heart, and so will every reader who becomes a part of its story

Cover photo was captured in Pune, Maharashtra

Find me on Instagram
@theroseveilpoetry

Hiraeth by Suhani Gamre

www.ingramcontent.com/pod-product-compliance
Lightning Source LLC
La Vergne TN
LVHW091116150826
845673LV00002B/852

* 9 7 9 8 8 9 7 2 4 1 1 5 6 *